It's Nice To Be Nice

April Allen

Illustrations by:
Eldon Jones III

Halo PUBLISHING INTERNATIONAL

ISBN: 978-1-61244-760-5
Library of Congress Control Number: 2019909203

Printed in the United States of America

Halo Publishing International
1100 NW Loop 410
Suite 700 - 176
San Antonio, Texas 78213
www.halopublishing.com
contact@halopublishing.com

To my father Vernon Brazzle who always told me, "It's nice to be nice." This advice has served me well from childhood to adulthood. Thank you for demonstrating what kindness looks like.

To my lady babies, Ella and Chloe. Never let anyone steal your joy or your smile. They did not give them to you, so they have no right to take them away.

I want to extend a special thank you to Donna Johnson. I am inspired by Donna's 26 years of freelance elementary school social work and social work management in the United Kingdom. Thank you for sharing your firsthand knowledge and expertise with me—understanding how to identify bullying, where it begins, and how to empower kids to stand up against it.

SCHOOL BUS

I couldn't wait to get to school today. I was excited to talk with my friends and play.

But today was different!

4

When I ran up to my friends, they were all so quiet, and they looked upset. I couldn't describe it.

I asked Ella, "You're so quiet. What is wrong?"

She said, "Someone at school told me not to sing my song!"

"What do you mean?" I asked. "I love when you sing, especially at your house on your karaoke machine."

Ella said, "Well, today Wyatt told me to be quiet!"

Then, he said, "Ella, stop singing that song. Your voice sounds bad, and the words are wrong."

Safiyyah said, "Then, Wyatt told me that he didn't like my clothes, so I couldn't join the game. He even told others to treat me the same."

Chloe then said, "Wyatt said something to me too. He said that he didn't like my hairdo."

I asked, "What did he say?"

8

Chloe answered, "First, he asked to see my hair, and he looked curious, but what he said next made me furious."

Hearing this, my face got super serious.

Chloe continued, "He told me my puffs were so big that if he looked inside he could probably find a baby pig. He said he was joking but it hurt my feelings really bad. He really made me feel sad."

"I am sorry he made you feel that way," I said. "Hurting others is never okay."

"Wyatt needs to learn a rule my dad taught me. My dad taught me 'It's nice to be nice, and before you speak, stop and think twice.'"

I know Wyatt because he is in my class. Sometimes, he is rude and even answers the teacher with a little sass.

One time I heard him make fun of Brice's hearing aid, but I told Brice that they were really cool and well-made.

I told Wyatt that those hearing aids help Brice to hear well, and because of them, we don't need to yell.

Once, I saw Wyatt hide Christine's eyeglasses, and he yelled at Catalina that she runs as slow as molasses.

After that, I went and told the teacher that Wyatt wasn't being very kind. The teacher made him sit in timeout on his behind.

The teacher talked to him about how it is not nice to talk to people in hurtful ways.

She told him that behavior would not be tolerated in class in any way.

I know it hurts when people act unkind and cruel.

These people don't seem to know my dad's kindness rule.

Ella said excitedly, "It's nice to be nice, and before you speak, stop and think twice."

Yes! That is it.

That is the rule that always helps me during the day a bit.

I have had my feelings hurt too. One kid used to say mean things about my hairdo.

But now saying mean things about my hair doesn't bother me at all, and I refuse to allow other people to make me feel small.

I guess it's because I love my hair, and I love how it feels. I love it so much because it stays in place when I do cartwheels.

It's cool that I am unique, and no one else looks exactly like me. I am beautiful and created perfectly.

If we all looked the same, you know how boring that would be.
The world wouldn't be as interesting and creative, don't you see?

It would be like having a box of crayons that were all the color white,
or to only see the sun but no stars at night.

It would be like everyone having the exact same shoes or everything
being the same shade of blue.

I had to learn that I am beautiful and special in every way, regardless of what other people might think or say.

What you need to remember is that you aren't ordinary. Just by being you, you are extraordinary.

Remember that when people are being mean, it's not about you. It's actually about them feeling blue.

People like Wyatt try to make us feel sad because deep down they are feeling really bad.

I know this is hard to believe, but my mom told me it's true.

Later during that day at school,
Wyatt passed by like he was really cool.

"Wyatt, you need to say you are sorry to my friends because I heard that you were unkind again!"

Chloe, Ella, and Safiyyah said, "And we have decided that we won't let you win!"

Ella said, "Today I made a choice to not let you silence my voice. I am proud of myself and inside I rejoice."

"I like to sing because it makes me feel happy inside. If you don't like it, you can go to the other side."

Chloe added, "If you don't like my hair, it doesn't matter to me, because it's beautiful in the mirrors I see."

Safiyyah said, "Wyatt, you need to learn Libby's golden rule. It's nice to be nice, and before you speak, stop and think twice."

Wyatt looked down and said, "Please forgive me. I know I shouldn't be mean, but sometimes I say those things because I don't feel seen."

He continued, "I don't want to be this way. I don't know what else to say."

"What you did was not okay," I said, "but we will give you another chance, starting today."

"You said enough, and we will forgive you, but if you play with us you must follow this rule too:

It's nice to be nice, and before you speak, stop and think twice."

Then, Wyatt came with us. He was kind and didn't fuss.

Before going to play, we even told the teacher what had happened just so she would know, and that day, all my friends felt their courage grow.

Wyatt soon learned we can all find something kind to say. We should try to do that with our friends every day.

And after that day, I often heard Wyatt say, "It's nice to be nice, and before I speak, I stop and think twice."

www.ingramcontent.com/pod-product-compliance
Lightning Source LLC
LaVergne TN
LVHW070839080426

835511LV00025B/3479